Dealing with Feeling...

Worried

Isabel Thomas

Illustrated by Clare Elsom

Chicago, Illinois

© 2013 Heinemann Library
an imprint of Capstone Global Library, LLC
Chicago, Illinois

Edited by Dan Nunn, Rebecca Rissman, and
  Catherine Veitch
Designed by Philippa Jenkins
Original illustrations © Clare Elsom
Illustrated by Clare Elsom
Production by Victoria Fitzgerald
Originated by Capstone Global Library, Ltd.
Printed in China

16 15 14 13 12
10 9 8 7 6 5 4 3 2 1

**Library of Congress Cataloging-in-Publication
Data**
Thomas, Isabel, 1980-
  Worried / Isabel Thomas.
    p. cm.—(Dealing with feeling)
  Includes bibliographical references and index.
  ISBN 978-1-4329-7110-6 (hb)—ISBN 978-1-
4329-7119-9 (pb) 1. Worry in children—Juvenile
literature. 2. Worry—Juvenile literature. I. Title.
  BF723.W67T56 2013
  152.4'6—dc23   2012008397

Contents

Some words are shown in bold, **like this.** Find out what they mean in the glossary on page 23.

What Is Worry?

worried

angry

caring

sad

Worry is a **feeling.** It is normal to have many kinds of feelings every day.

Some feelings are not nice to have. Worry is not a nice feeling. We feel worried when we think something bad might happen.

What Does It Feel Like to Be Worried?

Sometimes we might feel worried for a short time. When you are **nervous**, it can feel like there are butterflies in your stomach.

Sometimes worries can be very strong and last for a long time. It can be difficult to stop thinking about them.

How Do We Know When Someone Is Worried?

Our faces and bodies can show other people how we are feeling. **Feelings** can change the way that people behave, too.

Some people get grumpy when they
are worried, even with their friends.
Other people try to hide their worries.
This can make them feel worse.

Is It Normal to Feel Worried?

Some changes are exciting. Others can make you feel worried. It is normal to feel worried about a big change, such as moving to a new house or school.

Take breaks from worrying by doing something you enjoy. There are other things you can do to help yourself feel better, too.

How Can I Deal with Worries?

Sometimes things you see on the Internet or television can make you feel scared. It can be hard to deal with worries on your own.

Ask a grown-up to **explain** what you have seen. Finding out more about something can make it feel less scary.

When somebody in your family gets sick, it can make you feel very worried. Talking about your worries can make you feel better.

A grown-up can help you understand what is going on. Sometimes the thoughts inside our heads are very different from what is really happening.

What If I Can't Talk About My Feelings?

Imagine you are worried because somebody is **bullying** you or your friend. You might be scared that telling a grown-up will make it worse.

Other times, it is hard to put **feelings** into words. Try drawing a picture of your worries instead, and show it to a grown-up whom you trust.

Why Should I Deal with Worries?

Keeping worries inside can make you feel worse. Worries can get in the way and stop you from enjoying fun things.

You might not be able to **concentrate** in school. The best way to deal with **feelings** is to talk about them.

How Can I Help Someone Who Is Feeling Worried?

Everyone feels worried sometimes, even grown-ups. When people you know are worried, they might want to talk about how they feel.

You can help by listening. Sometimes, just sharing worries with someone makes the worries go away.

21

Make a Worry Toolbox

Write down some tips to help you deal with worried **feelings.**

Find out more about the thing that is worrying you.

Take your mind off worrying by reading a book or listening to music.

Think to think happy thoughts.

Help yourself to feel less worried about a big event by practicing as much as you can.

Take a few deep breaths.

Go for a walk or a run.

Share your worries with people you trust. Get their ideas and help.

Draw a picture of the things that make you feel worried.

Glossary

bullying when a person harms or is nasty to somebody

concentrate focus all your attention on something, so that you can do it well

explain describe something in a way that makes it easier to understand

feeling something that happens inside our minds. It can affect our bodies and the way we behave.

nervous scared or worried about doing something

Find Out More

Books

Henkes, Kevin. *Wemberly Worried.*
  New York: Greenwillow, 2010.
Medina, Sarah. *Worried (Feelings).*
  Chicago: Heinemann Library, 2007.
Wolff, Ferida. *Is a Worry Worrying You?*
  Terre Haute, Ind.: Tanglewood, 2007.

Internet sites

Facthound offers a safe, fun way to find Internet sites related to this book. All of the sites on Facthound have been researched by our staff.

Here's all you do:
Visit www.facthound.com
Type in this code: 9781432971106

Index